Technology Safety

BY SUSAN KESSELRING   ILLUSTRATED BY DAN McGEEHAN

Published by The Child's World®
800-599-READ • childsworld.com

Copyright © 2025 by The Child's World®
All rights reserved. No part of this book may be reproduced or utilized in any form or by any means without written permission from the publisher.

ISBN Information
9781503894013 (Reinforced Library Binding)
9781503895102 (Portable Document Format)
9781503895928 (Online Multi-user eBook)
9781503896741 (Electronic Publication)

LCCN
2024942721

Printed in the United States of America

ABOUT THE AUTHOR
Susan Kesselring loves children, books, nature, and her family. She teaches K-1 students in a progressive charter school down a little country lane in Castle Rock, Minnesota. She is the mother of five daughters and lives in Apple Valley, Minnesota with her husband and a crazy springer spaniel named Lois Lane.

ABOUT THE ILLUSTRATOR
Dan McGeehan spent his younger years as an actor, author, playwright, and editor. Now he spends his days drawing, and he is much happier.

TABLE OF CONTENTS

CHAPTER ONE
Safety with Technology . . . 4

CHAPTER TWO
Phone Rules . . . 7

CHAPTER THREE
Video Game Safety . . . 8

CHAPTER FOUR
Watching TV . . . 11

CHAPTER FIVE
Safety Online . . . 12

CHAPTER SIX
Passwords . . . 16

Technology Safety Rules . . . 20
Wonder More . . . 21
Internet Safety Traffic Light . . . 22
Glossary . . . 23
Find Out More . . . 24
Index . . . 24

Chapter 1

Safety with Technology

How do you use **technology**? Do you email your best friend on the computer? Do you text a lot on the phone? Are you great at video games?

All this technology helps us learn about the world, keep in touch with each other, and have fun. But it's important to know a few rules that will keep you safe.

Hi! I'm Buzz B. Safe. Watch for me! I'll show you how to be safe with technology.

CHAPTER 2

Phone Rules

Technology is the use of science, skills, and ideas to make new or better things. Machines are made that solve problems or make life easier. A phone is an example of technology. It solves the problem of how to talk to people who are not nearby.

Each family has its own rules about using the phone. Do you have your own phone? Perhaps it is a **smartphone**. When is it okay for you to use it? What should you say when you answer a call? When is it okay to text your friends? Just ask your parents.

CHAPTER 3

Video Game Safety

Video games are another form of technology that can be lots of fun. Some games help you learn. Maybe you've even played a video game in school!

But not all video games are great. Some show things you shouldn't see. Really violent war games are probably not good to play. Talk with your parents about which video games you are allowed to play. Avoid spending all your time gaming, though! Get outside and play with friends, too. Fresh air and active fun keeps you healthy.

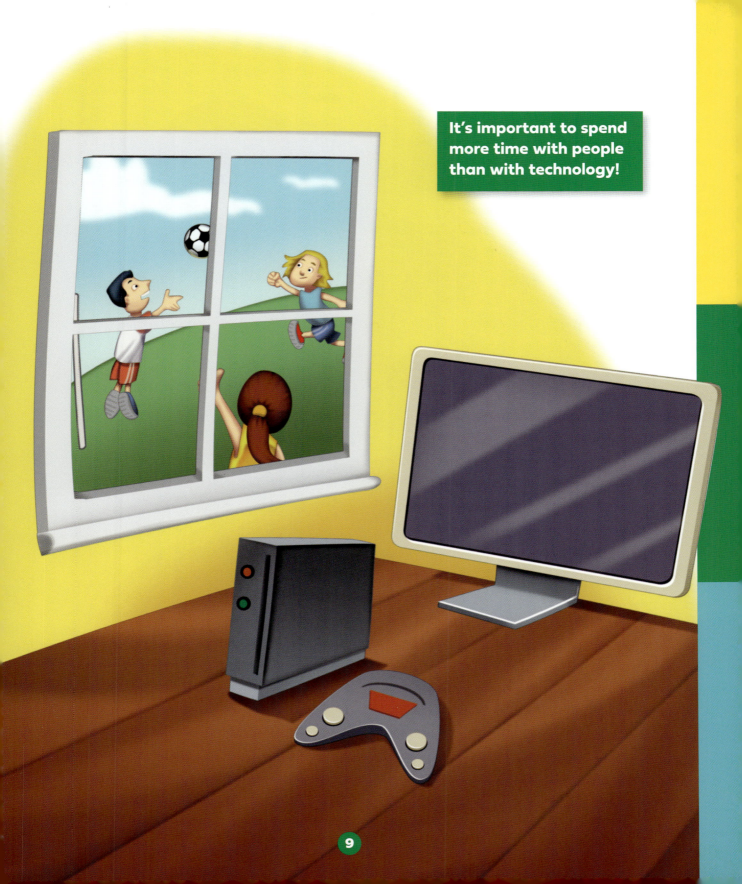

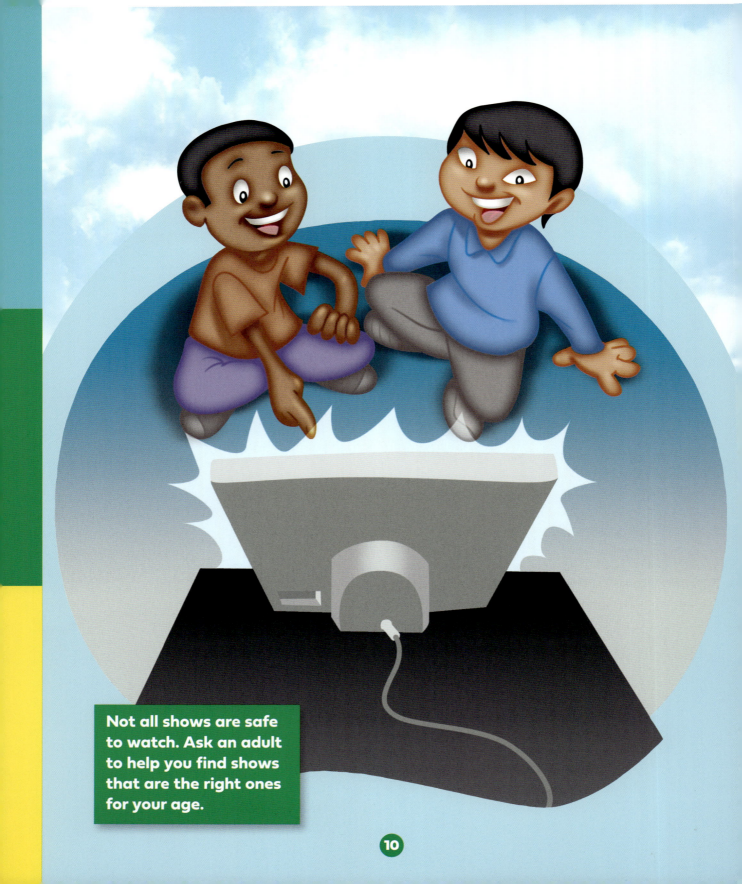

Not all shows are safe to watch. Ask an adult to help you find shows that are the right ones for your age.

CHAPTER 4

Watching TV

You can learn a lot from watching television. You can learn lots of new things. Shows are entertaining, too!

But check with your parents before watching. Some shows are not good for kids. And avoid watching any screen for too long. You'll miss out on other things—like swinging and playing basketball! Plan out the shows you will watch each week. Then stick to your plan.

Avoid getting stuck in front of the screen! Limit what you watch—on your phone and your TV— to no more than two hours each day.

CHAPTER 5
Safety Online

A computer is like a really big brain—it can store so much information. That makes it a great learning tool. When it's connected to the Internet, you can find out almost anything you want to know. A computer also helps you stay in touch with friends. To use it safely, though, you need to know some important rules.

When you're **online**, you can visit websites about almost anything. Try clicking your **mouse** on certain spots on the computer screen. The spots are called **links**. They lead you to other information you want to know—like cool facts about Mars or fun math games.

Having a parent nearby when you're online can help keep you safe.

But clicking on the wrong link can cause problems for your computer. It could also bring you to a website that isn't for kids. Always have a parent near you when you are on the Internet. They can tell you if it is safe to click.

People are not always honest when they tell people about themselves online. Be sure you always have an adult nearby when going online.

On some websites, people can send you messages. You know to be careful around strangers. But on the computer, it is tricky to tell who is a stranger and who is a friend. Some people may pretend to be people they are not. Tell your parents about all of your online friends. And never plan to meet an online friend without your mom or dad.

Social media sites, such as TikTok, Snapchat, and Instagram, can be fun, but very dangerous. Always have an adult's permission and guidance to use such sites.

CHAPTER 6

Passwords

Just to be safe, some information needs to be kept **private**. Avoid putting your name, picture, age, phone number, and address on the Internet. Also, if you type this information into a public computer, other people might be able to see it. Have your parent check the site out first. And, keep computer **passwords** private, too.

Keeping your passwords in a notebook that's kept in a safe place is a good idea.

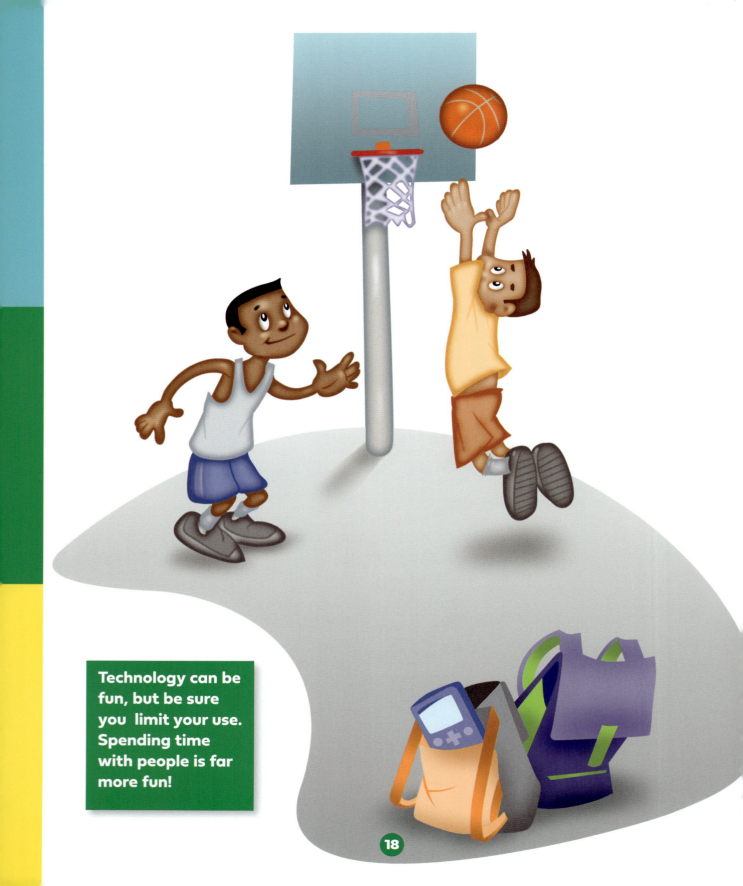

Technology can be fun, but be sure you limit your use. Spending time with people is far more fun!

Remember that technology is cool, but it is also just a tool. People, not technology, should be your best friends. Be sure to spend time having fun with friends and family! Use technology wisely and make time for other fun things in your life.

Never be mean or embarrass others online. If someone bullies YOU online, tell an adult right away.

Technology Safety Rules

- Talk with your parents about how and when to use your phone.
- Check with your parents about which video games are good for you.
- With your parents, plan which television shows to watch.
- Watch no more than two hours of television each day.
- Always have your mom or dad near you when you are online.
- Tell your parents about your online friends.
- Keep your name, age, address, phone number, and passwords private.
- Remember to spend most of your time with people, not technology.

Wonder More

Wondering about New Information

How much did you know about safely using technology before you read this book? What new information did you learn? Write down three new facts that this book taught you. Was the new information surprising? Why or why not?

Wondering How It Matters

What would you do if you came across something online that made you feel uncomfortable or scared?

Wondering Why

Why is it important to limit your screen time and use of technology? Explain your answer.

Ways to Keep Wondering

After reading this book, what questions do you have about technology safety? What can you do to learn more about it?

Internet Safety Traffic Light

Make this craft to identify safe, cautious, and dangerous online situations.

You will need:
- Construction paper (red, yellow, green, and black)
- Scissors
- Glue stick or tape
- Markers, crayons, or colored pencils

Instructions:

1. Cut a large rectangle from the black construction paper. This is will be the base of your traffic light.

2. Cut out one circle from the red, yellow, and green construction paper. Use your glue stick or tape to stick them onto the black rectangle.

3. In each section, write examples of online activities that go with that color. Remember green is "good," yellow is "caution," and red is "stop."

Glossary

Internet (IN-tur-net): The Internet is the system that allows many computers to connect to each other. You can find a lot of information on the Internet.

links (LINGKS): Links are pictures or words you click on to get to another part of the Internet. Ask your parents if you're not sure if you should click on certain links.

mouse (MOWSS): A mouse is a small oval-shaped tool that you move with your hand to control what happens on your computer screen. Ask your parents before using your mouse to click on a link.

online (on-LYN): Online describes being on the Internet. Ask your parents the rules about going online.

passwords (PASS-wurds): Passwords are secret codes. Sometimes you need passwords to get on your computer or to visit places on the Internet.

private (PRY-vit): If something is private, it is not to be shared with strangers. Keep your computer passwords private.

smartphone (SMART-fohn): A smartphone is a phone and computer in one device. Smartphones allow users to call people, use email, play games, and use the Internet.

social media (SOH-shul MEE-dee-yuh): Social media is the name for the forms of electronic communication, such as websites or applications, where users share information, personal messages, and other content.

technology (tek-NOL-uh-jee): Technology is a thing that solves a problem and is made using science. Computers and phones are examples of technology.

Find Out More

In the Library

Du Thaler, Nina. *Tom Tames His Online World: Cyber Safety Can Be Fun (Diary of Elle series)*. Brisbane, Australia: Bright Zebra, 2017.

Herman, Steve. *Teach Your Dragon Online Safety: A Story About Navigating the Internet Safely and Responsibly*. Houston, TX: DG Books, 2023.

Rovanesi, Olimena J.M. *Be Safe Online*. Independently Published, 2024.

On the Web

Visit our Web site for links about technology safety:

childsworld.com/links

Note to Parents, Teachers, and Librarians: We routinely verify our Web links to make sure they are safe and active sites. So encourage your readers to check them out!

Index

computers, 4, 12, 13, 15, 16,
email, 4
friends, 4, 7, 8, 12, 15, 19
fun, 4, 8, 12, 15, 18, 19
healthy, 8
information, 12, 16
Internet, 12, 13,16

learning, 4, 8, 11, 12
links, 12, 13
parents, 5, 7, 8, 11, 13, 15, 16
people, 7, 9, 14, 15, 16, 18, 19
passwords, 16, 17
phones, 4, 6, 7, 11, 16

science, 7
screens, 11, 12
shows, 10, 11
strangers, 15
television, 11
text, 4, 7
video games, 4, 8

24